Comprehensive
Teaching Models
in
Social Studies
Education

Comprehensive
Teaching Models
in
Social Studies
Education

David Zodikoff

State University of New York
College at Cortland

KENDALL/HUNT PUBLISHING COMPANY
DUBUQUE, IOWA

Contents

CHAPTER 1

Introduction of Meaning and Uses
of Various Models

This text is designed for college students and teachers in social studied education, in both pre-service and in-service education courses. Actually, this book is an attempt to put actual college teaching experiences into written form. Therefore, the sequential pattern of the text follows the presentation used by the author in his undergraduate and graduate classes in social studies education.

Unlike most social studies methods books, this text tries to combine important concepts, skills, and social attitudes into an interrelated unit that selects content as a means to achieve a unified comprehensive end. Each of the four models described in this chapter are so structured to aid the teacher and student to better organize their learning goals into more organized comprehensive patterns. This is particularly true of the comprehensive model outline which is used to illustrate teaching topics on elementary and secondary school levels.

One of the most frequently heard criticisms of social studies instruction is that the learning is too fragmentary, and that the learning goals seem to be only concerned with the memorization of unrelated facts and concepts. Although the models presented in this text offer no panaceas for such problems, they should aid both the teacher and student to better organize their concepts and materials to achieve more meaningful balanced learning.

Three published articles are included in this chapter to supply some background into the thought stages that led to the organization and use of the comprehensive model outline. The point should be made here that the structure found in any of the models should be used in as flexible a manner as possible. Many college students that have been exposed to these models found that they could plan and teach certain content easier by combining various concepts, attitudes or skills, instead of treating them separately as depicted in the various basic model outlines. This is fine and should be encouraged to those adopting these models for teaching purposes, for whatever structure makes the most sense to the teacher will probably result in more successful teaching and learning.

A STUDY OF SOCIAL ATTITUDES OF FOURTH, FIFTH AND SIXTH GRADE PUPILS

The attitudes of the children of the next generation will be of great significance in determining the future of this country. Therefore attitudes should be of great concern to this country's educators. If we find that a relationship exists between attitudes held by children, and certain easily identifiable variables, this may give us clues regarding areas of particular need for educational programs designed to modify or reinforce attitudes.

The main purpose of this study was to discover by developing a scale of social attitudes any relationships between certain backgrounds of children, and some of the attitudes perhaps generally considered most vital in a democracy. Attitudes in the study were categorized within the following behavioral areas: democratic living, group interdependence, empathy, independent thinking, and social responsibility.

The five behavioral areas selected for this study were derived from the several sources that advocated the school's use of attitudes considered the most vital in a democracy. Hunnicutt listed seven basic behavioral schemes. These schemes included: (1) People's manner of living is a product of environmental interaction, (2) In search of progress, people have built a constantly changing panorama of culture and cililization, (3) People work, invent, and build to satisfy their changing needs and desires, (4) People strive for order and justice through law and government, (5) Through sharing experiences, people learn to live together, (6) People need enrichment for their daily existence and (7) People increasingly recognize their interdependence with all mankind, and must share responsibility for the general welfare.[1] The Social Studies Curriculum Center of Syracuse University stressed five value attitude areas. These attitude areas include: (1) The Dignity of Man or the need for students to respect the individual rights of others, (2) Empathy, which can't be just taught, but taught and practiced as a behavioral value, so that students that accept this value will practice it, (3) Loyality, or the learning of which loyalties are right and which are wrong, and how to test, effectively, certain positive loyalties to one's people and country, (4) Government by the Consent of the Governed, which would overlap with the previous mentioned attitude areas, and (5) Freedom and Equality, which also overlaps with the above attitude areas, and includes knowledge and practice of freedom with responsibility and respect for other's equality.[2] The Bureau of Curriculum Development of the New York State Education Department advocated the following key attitude areas: (1) Interdependence, whereby people become social through group life and shared experiences, (2) Adaptation-Conservation, in which people's lives are conditioned by their natural environment, (3) Cooperation, whereby people work together to satisfy their needs and desires, (4) Democracy, where people try, through mutually accepted laws and organization, to gain justice and security, and (5) Progress, whereby people have struggled through time to achieve a better life.[3] Michaelis has also stressed the use of such attitude areas as interdependence, independent thinking, and other social skills development necessary to train children to live in a deomocracy.[4]

From the above sources of major attitude areas, the attitude areas of group cooperation, democratic living, independentt thinking, empathy, and social responsibility have been selected for use in this study. Group cooperation is defined as expressed attitudes involving how well one feels about working with others. Democratic living is defined as attitudes in regard to favorable or unfavorable expressed feelings toward respect for other people's equal rights. Independent thinking is defined as attitudes expressive of one's desire to think on a more independent level. Empathy is defined as expressed attitudes relating to how well one person relates with another person's feelings. Social responsibility is defined as attitudes related to the child's respect for his individual obligations to obey the rules of the home, school, and community.

Method

A list of 50 positive attitude items were comprised that were relevant to each of the five attitude areas. Eighteen graduate students in education, with previous teaching experience at the elementary school level, were asked to place the 50 positive items under the 5 relevant attitude areas. Attitude statements that showed a very clear majority in their placement were retained. Those that did not have a clear majority were discarded and the 25 positive statements, five in each area, that were most consistently chosen made up the intial questionnaire. These 25 positive statements were also expressed in a negative manner so that the questionnaire contained 5 positive and 5 negative statements under each of the 5 attitude areas. This initial questionnaire was then administered to a sample 4th grade class and a final revision was made.[5]

The questionnaire was then administered to 70 fourth grade pupils, 87 fifth grade pupils, and 88 sixth grade pupils. Each of the three grades represented a wide range of I.Q. and achievement levels. The Lorge-Thorndike Intelligence Test and Kuhlman-Anderson Achievement Test were the measuring instruments used in the study. The mean I.Q. for the three grades was 102 in fourth grade, 103 in fifth grade, and 106 in sixth grade. The mean achievement level was 3.8 in fourth grade, 4.8 in fifth grade, and 6.0 in sixth grade. The subjects were all from a lower-middle to upper-middle class socio-economic level. The five positively-oriented and five negatively-oriented statements included in the questionnaire for each area were scattered throughout the questionnaire to avoid mechanical responses or possible halo effects.

The basic data consisted of the student's responses to the fifty items on the questionnaire. A five-point grading scale was used in computing the data. Positively-oriented statements were scaled from 1/ for strongly agree, 2/ mildly agree, 3/ don't really care, 4/ mildly disagree, to 5/ strongly disagree. Negatively-oriented statements were scaled from 5/ for strongly disagree to 1/ for strongly agree. This was done so each negative statement was the reverse of each positive statement.

Results

A major hypothesis of the study was that students with above-average achievement would have significantly higher positive attitude scores than students with below-average achievement. Controlled variables were sex, I.Q. and grade level. The results of Table I support the hypothesis that students with above-average achievement at each grade level would have significantly higher favorable attitude scores than students with below-average achievement. Other hypotheses sought significant differences between students when either sex, I.Q. or grade level were considered the independent variables. In all cases, between sexes, grades, or I.Q. level, no significant differences were found between total positive attitude scores.

TABLE I

**Comparison of Positive Attitude Scores Between Pupils
of High and Low Achievement at Each Grade Level**

Grade	N	High Achv't. $\bar{X}$	S.D.	Low Achv't. $\bar{X}$	S.D.	t
5 Girls	30	213	8	192	13	7 $<$ .001
5 Girls	24	214	12	178	26	4.1 $<$ .01
4 Girls	22	212	9	183	13	7.3 $<$ .01
6 Boys	30	213	9	184	18	4.1 $<$ .01
5 Boys	24	210	10	180	15	6 $<$ .01
4 Boys	22	200	15	160	12	8 $<$ .001

Table II compares the total weighted mean attitude scores, by each grade level. Of particular interest is the fact that independent thinking received the lowest favorable attitude score at each grade level. It's an interesting observation because many educational sources, found by the writer, claimed that critical or independent thinking was one of the major goals of elementary school programs.

TABLE II

Total Grade Weighted Mean Attitude
Scores for Five Attitude Areas

Attitude Area	(N70) Grade 4	(N87) Grade 5	(N83) Grade 6
Group Cooperation	493	656	663
Sympathy	559	694	748
Independent Thinking	462	597	609
Social Responsibility	567	685	715
Democratic Living	550	670	724
Average Grade Means	526	660	692
s.d.	41	34	50

Order of Attitude Areas, By Grade, From Most to Least Popular

Grade 4	Grade 5	Grade 6
Social Responsibility	Empathy	Empathy
Sympathy	Social Responsibility	Democratic Living
Democratic Living	Democratic Living	Social Responsibility
Group Cooperation	Group Cooperation	Group Cooperation
Independent Thinking	Independent Thinking	Independent Thinking

Summary of Conclusions

This study tested the relationship between the positive attitudes expressed by nine-to-eleven-year-old children in fourth grades through sixth grades compared with the student's sex, I.Q. achievement, and grade level. The only significant relationship found was between students of above- and below-average achievement at each grade level with I.Q. and sex being the controlled variables. Although Table I shows that students with above-average achievement had significantly higher favorable attitude scores than students with below-average achievement at each grade level, the study did not disclose whether the student's high achievement caused a high positive attitude score, or if the reverse was true. Future studies could apply the same questionnaire on a pretest and post-test basis, using a variety of methods or techniques.

Another result of the study showed no significant relationship between sexes of children, children of above- and below-average I.Q. levels, or children of different grade levels when the variables of sex, I.Q. and achievement were held constant. This offers an opportunity for a future study to add a variable consisting of various teacher personalities and their possible influence on pupil attitude change in their classrooms.

It was also mentioned that of the five attitude areas, independent thinking had the lowest positive attitude score at each grade level. This would seem to imply that a more positive attitude could result in this area if classroom teachers planned and encouraged more daily heuristic activities for their children.

At the present time, this attitude questionnaire is being utilized in over 50 fifth grade teachers inconjunction with the use of a new course—Jerome Bruner's Man: A Course of Study—to determine what, if any, attitude changes can be found by the end of the school year in comparison to the results of student reactions to the questionnaire prior to undertaking the new study.

INSTRUCTIONS: After you read each statement carefully, check one of the boxes at the right that tells how you feel about each statement.

	strongly disagree	mildly disagree	don't really care	mildly agree	strongly agree
1. I would usually prefer to work with others than to work alone.					
2. I feel sorry when someone is treated unfairly.					
3. I like to try to solve new problems by myself.					
4. I usually report students who have broken school rules.					
5. I think other people should have the same rights as I do.					
6. The friends I like best are the ones who think the way I do.					
7. I wish some of my classmates had nicer homes and clothes.					
8. I become very nervous when I can't find quick answers to problems.					
9. I try to tell my friends to obey school laws.					
10. I think a citizen should obey all laws.					
11. I want some friends who think differently from me.					

	strongly disagree	mildly disagree	don't really care	mildly agree	strongly agree
12. I like to help other children having trouble with school work.					
13. I like a teacher always to tell me just how to do things.					
14. I obey signs that tell me to stay off someones' property.					
15. I would rather be told what rules to obey, than have to help in making up rules.					
16. I usually prefer to work alone rather than with others.					
17. I am sorry for children who work hard in school and still get low marks.					
18. I like it when the teacher lets us search in books for hard answers.					
19. I only obey laws that I like.					
20. I like it when my teacher lets us help to make class rules.					
21. Group work is more interesting than working alone.					
22. It doesn't bother me when someone else is treated unfairly.					

	strongly disagree	mildly disagree	don't really care	mildly agree	strongly agree
23. I like to take toys apart to see how they work.					
24. I often like to do things behind the teacher's back.					
25. I like it when I have more freedom than my classmates.					
26. I like playing games alone rather than with others.					
27. When someone loses a game to me, I like to tell him how I played better.					
28. I like to try to solve hard puzzles.					
29. It's usually alright to cheat if you don't get caught.					
30. I think a good leader is one who does the things I like.					
31. I like to play in team games rather than play alone.					
32. When someone loses a game to me, I usually tell him how well he played.					
33. I don't enjoy working at hard puzzles.					
34. I usually try to obey rules.					

	strongly disagree	mildly disagree	don't really care	mildly agree	strongly agree
35. My teacher and parents should try to teach me to be fair with other people.					
36. I think it's more important to be the star player than to try to help my team win.					
37. I don't like children who don't have as nice homes or clothes as I do.					
38. I don't like to make up poems or draw pictures.					
39. I don't care if other children break school rules.					
40. A good leader must want to be fair with everyone.					
41. I like to share my ideas with others in group work.					
42. I'm glad when other children get lower marks in school than I.					
43. The only children I try to be fair with are my friends.					
44. I think that many children should have beliefs different from mine.					

	strongly disagree	mildly disagree	don't really care	mildly agree	strongly agree
45. I like it when my teacher treats me better than my classmates.					
46. I think it's more important to help my team win than to try to be the star of the team.					
47. I only like to help children who are my close friends.					
48. Other children's rights are not as important as mine.					
49. I only obey my parents when I like what they ask me to do.					
50. I usually don't like to share my ideas with others.					

List of Major Behavioral Areas and Related Attitude Statements

The number preceding each attitude statement denotes its position on the questionnaire.

Group Cooperation

Attitude Statement

1. I would usually prefer to work with others than to work alone.
21. Group work is more interesting than working alone.
31. I like to play in team games rather than to play alone.

41. I like to share my ideas with others in group work.

46. I think it's more important to help my team win than to try to be the star of the team.

16. I usually prefer to work alone rather than with others.

26. I like playing games alone rather than with others.

36. I think it's more important to be the star player than to try to help my team win.

50. I usually don't like to share my ideas with others.

15. I would rather be told what rules to obey, than have to help in making up rules.

Empathy

Attitude Statement

2. I feel sorry when someone is treated unfairly.

7. I wish some of my classmates had nicer homes and clothes.

12. I like to help other children having trouble with schoolwork.

17. I am sorry for children who work hard in school and still get low marks.

32. When someone loses a game to me, I usually tell him how well he played.

22. It doesn't bother me when someone else is treated unfairly.

27. When someone loses a game to me, I like to tell him how I played better.

37. I don't like children who don't have as nice homes or clothes as I do.

42. I'm glad when other children get lower marks in school than I.

47. I only like to help children who are my close friends.

Independent Thinking

Attitude Statement

3. I like to try to solve new problems by myself.

11. I want some friends who think differently from me.

18. I like it when the teacher lets us search in books for hard answers.

23. I like to take toys apart to see how they work.

28. I like to try to solve hard puzzles.

6. The friends I like best are the ones who think the way I do.

8. I become very nervous when I can't find quick answers to problems.

13. I like a teacher always to tell me just how to do things.

33. I don't enjoy working at hard puzzles.

38. I don't like to make up poems or draw pictures.

Social Responsibility

Attitude Statement

4. I usually report students who have broken school rules.

9. I try to tell my friends to obey school laws.

10. I think a citizen should obey all laws.

14. I obey laws that I like.

34. I usually try to obey rules.

19. I only obey laws that I like.

24. I often like to do things behind the teacher's back.

29. It's usually alright to cheat if you don't get caught.

39. I don't care if other children break school rules.

49. I only obey my parents when I like what they ask me to do.

Democratic Living

Attitude Statement

5. I think other people should have the same rights as I do.

20. I like it when my teacher lets us help make class rules.

35. My teacher and parents should try to teach me to be fair with other people.

40. A good leader must want to be fair with everyone.

44. I think that many children should have beliefs different from mine.

25. I like it when I have more freedom than my classmates.

30. I think a good leader is one who does the things I like.
45. I like it when my teacher treats me better than my classmates.
43. The only children I try to be fair with are my friends.
48. Other children's rights are not as important as mine.

Bibliography

1. Bureau of Elementary Curriculum Development, New York State Education Department, Albany, 1961, 87 pp.

2. Hunnicutt, C.W., *We Look Around Us,* Syracuse, The L.W. Singer Co., 1963, 218 pp.

3. Michaelis, John U., *Social Studies for Children in a Democracy,* New York, Prentice-Hall, Inc., 1950, 466 pp.

4. Price, Roy A., Gerald R. Smith and Warren L. Hickman, *Major Concepts for the Social Studies,* Syracuse, Syracuse University Press, 1965, 62 pp.

5. Zodikoff, David H., "A Study of Categories of Social Attitudes Fourth, Fifth and Sixth Grade Pupils." School of Education, Syracuse University, June, 1967, 147 pp., Published in *Research in Education,* U.S. Office of Education, September 1971.

SUGGESTED MODELS FOR
DEVELOPING SOCIAL STUDIES COMPREHENSION

The three instructional models, included in this report, have been developed by the author with his students in a pre-service social studies course for college juniors that are education majors. All three of these models are structured as types of heuristic paradigms. That is, there are many different types of content that can be included within relevant areas. A basic value of these models is that teachers are offered a structural design **before**, as well as during, their teaching efforts. Also, in the area of evaluation, it would seem that teachers can more clearly define learning success if they have identified specific conceptual, attitude, and skill areas.

Figure 1 is an attitude-content model that the author has used with many undergraduates for open-ended discussion purposes. The basic use of this model requires the relevant connection of specific content from various social science disciplines with a specific attitude. The five attitude areas in the model have the following operational definitions:

1. social responsibility or respect for obligation to obey the rules of the home, school, and community.

2. independent thinking or the desire to think on more individual level.

3. democratic living or the growth of improved attitudes toward increasing respect for other people's equal rights.

4. empathy or developing the ability to relate and identify more closely with other people's situations.

5. group cooperation or developing more favorable attitudes toward working more effectively with others.[1]

Each of the topics in the model are broad and open-ended to encourage continuous research and assimilation. Teachers should develop these attitudes in the meaning sense defined by Edwards and Remmers. Edwards defined an attitude as "the degree of positive or negative feeling expressed about some psychological object."[2] Remmers defined an attitude as "a felt idea or group of ideas which sets persons to act in relation to specific objects that arouse such feelings."[3]

As a result of an attitude questionnaire study dealing with the five mentioned attitude areas administered to 245 fourth, fifth and sixth grade children, the attitude of independent thinking had the lowest favorable attitude score in comparison with the other four attitude areas. Therefore, the use of such a model as shown in Figure 1 might help to develop more favorable attitudes in children and their teachers.

Figures 2 and 3 have been used with same structural rationale as Figure 1. That is, specific concepts and skills have been related to appropriate content from the various social sciences. Ideally, the skills model should be interwoven, meaningfully with the attitudes and concepts models.

Allport defined a concept as "any intellectualized category on any given understood mental level, by the learner, and that any concept has both an emotional and/or intellectual level of comprehension."[4] It is vital that teachers of young children are aware of this dual comprehension level of concepts, as children learn something first on an affective level, and learn to intellectualize or apply verbal labels at later maturity. In the elementary school social studies programs, children in the early primary grades can develop democratic attitudes in a classroom before they can verbalize the meaning of these experiences. If teachers waited until children could verbalize such abstract terms, then it may be too late. Although no complete panaceas are claimed for any of these models, they should promote greater intellectual and emotional growth, if used by teachers who are willing to innovate and change themselves.

	Social Responsibility	Independent Thinking	Democratic Living	Empathy	Group Cooperation
History	Constitution and its demands	Civil disobedience	Rural-urban living	Feelings for Immigrants	Westward expansion
Geography	Laws of Nature and laws of man	How to improve land	Utilitarianism	Aid to underdeveloped countries	Imperial Valley
Sociology	Group interdependence and work in social groups	Possible reformed class system	How can groups function better	Welfare Laws	Rigidity of social order
Economics	Careful use of money	How to avoid inflation	Concept of exploitation	Government supports	Balanced Economy
Political Science	Proper use of authority	How do governments vary	Study of civil disobedience	Rights of all citizens	Rights and respect of individual citizens

Figure 1. Attitudes Model

History

1. Past events cause present conditions in history.
2. Great leaders helped change their times as well as being affected by them.
3. Certain events in history can drastically change future directions.

Geography

1. Man and his physical environment are interdependent.
2. The location of an area greatly determines the people's way of life.
3. Natural resources are distributed unevenly around the world.

Political Science

1. In a democracy, people help to make laws.
2. Certain laws are necessary if a society is to function.
3. Our American government works on a checks and balance system.

Economics

1. As prices rise, the **real** value of a dollar goes down.
2. When demand exceeds supply, the cost of goods will be high.
3. Conservation of natural resources helps a country to stay strong.

Sociology

1. The family is a primary social human institution.
2. American society is made up of many different ethnic, social and economic groups.
3. In an open society, a person can rise socially by his ability, unlike a closed society where social status is determined by birth rather than ability.

Figure 2. Concepts Model

1. History—structure—study the relationships between past persons, times, and events.

   skills—(a) ability to differentiate primary and secondary sources.
   (b) ability to critically evaluate validity of sources.
   (c) ability to judge ideas or studied evidence rather than opinion.
   (d) ability to write brief biographies without eulogizing or debunking.
   (e) ability to interpret and write time-line charts.

2. Geography—structure—approach by culture, physical location, economic wealth, political name.

   skills—(a) to locate specific areas of the world.
   (b) to define and apply technical terms such as latitude, longitude, hemisphere and others.
   (c) to demonstrate the use of scale and key on maps.
   (d) to define and apply the concept of distortion and different uses of homolosine mercator, polar maps.
   (e) to explain the effect of location on climate and types of living.

3. Political Science—structure—local, state, national, international political structures.

   skills—(a) how and why governments at each level are so organized.
   (b) how checks and balances system operates and its advantages and disadvantages.
   (c) to contrast, types of government such as dictatorship, democracy, monarchy.
   (d) to define and apply parts and function of the constitution.
   (e) the meaning of citizenship including rights and duties.

4. Economics—structure—approach by individual, local, state, national, international economic problem areas.

   skills—(a) to define and apply key terms such as Gross National Product, money income, real income, and theory of supply and demand.
   (b) how the areas of government and economics are interdependent.
   (c) how the areas of geography and economics are interdependent.
   (d) how the areas of sociology and economics are interdependent.
   (e) what attitudes in terms of economics and its uses affect our social classes.

5. Sociology.

   skills—(a) to differentiate folkways and mores and give contrasting examples.
   (b) to list and interrelate each of the social sciences for a **total** culture view.
   (c) to identify areas of social stratification and explain various social roles.
   (d) to relate the types of formal education to social effects. (conservative—progressive)
   (e) to explain how the art, music, literature, relate to a total life culture.

Figure 3. Skills Model

Bibliography

1. Zodikoff, David, "A Questionnaire Scale Study of Social Attitudes of Intermediate Grade Children," *Counseling and Personnel Services Information Center*, University of Michigan, Ann Arbor, Michigan, March 1970, ERIC Clearinghouse Document Number CG 005 673 or *Research in Education*, December, 1970.

2. Edwards, Allen L., *Techniques of Attitude Scale Construction*, New York, Appleton-Century-Crofts, Inc., 1957, 256 pp.

3. Remmers, H.H., *Introduction to Opinion and Attitude Measurement*, New York, Harper and Brothers, 1954, 431 pp.

4. Allport, Gordon W., *The Nature of Prejudice*, New York, Doubleday and Co., Inc., 1958, 496 pp.

THE USE OF COMPREHENSIVE MODELS IN
SOCIAL STUDIES INSTRUCTION

The instructional models included in this report have been developed and discussed with several hundred undergraduate education majors. On the basis of their anonymous written course evaluations, a significant majority of these students found the models to be heuristic and provocative enough to result in meaningful class discussion over a prolonged period of time. More important, it is believed that these models are flexible enough to be used in **both** elementary and secondary level social studies programs.

A frequent criticism heard of public school social studies programs is that the facts and concepts are presented in a fragmented and disconnected manner. Therefore, both learning and evaluation rarely leave the memorization level of cognitive retention. Another criticism is that little **deliberate** attention is given by teachers to the student's affective or emotional development. These models have been developed as at least an attempt to combine relevant factual and conceptual knowledge with a pre-planned teacher effort to correlate these cognititve learnings with specific attitude development on the affective level.

Each of these models connects specific concepts, skills, and attitudes within one or more specified social science areas. It is recommended that teachers write out these complete models **before** they teach, so they can at least begin with some basic connected structure. The point must also be made that these models are heuristic enough that a wide variety of content, skills, and attitudes could be integrated within them. Therefore, the model structure remains the same, but with great flexibility of its usage.

Although no claim is made here that these models are a panacea for faulty social studies instruction, the belief is strongly held that these models should develop more meaningful and creative learning of human phenomena on the part of both the teacher and student. The enclosed models will have more meaning to the reader if he first studies the sources listed in the bibliography.[1] . [2] . [3] . [4]

Model One

Social Science Area and Concept—History—Past events cause present conditions in our society. Example—current Civil Rights issues.

Specific Skills

1. Study primary source documents pertaining to slavery, Indian affairs and other minority groups.
2. Develop criteria for determining validity of sources.
3. Construct a sequential cause-effect time line chart include key dates such as 1619, 1789, 1865.

Attitudes Relevant to Topic

1. **empathy**—Feelings toward minority groups in American culture.
2. **independent thinking**—Stress value of ideas based on evidence rather than just opinion.
3. **social responsibility**—Compare and contrast the union and confederate governments.
4. **democratic living**—Where was and is the respect for the rights of others violated?
5. **group cooperation**—Study the role played by the underground railroad in the abolitionist movement.

Model Two

Social Science Area and Concept—Geography—An area's physical location greatly determines the way people live.

Specific Skills

1. Apply technical geographical terms to specifically locate and describe an area.
2. The use of basic map parts to draw general inferences of a given area.
3. By use of map skills and technical geographic terms relate why an area has its climate, topography, and ways of living.

Attitudes Relevant to Topic

1. **empathy**—To identify with people of various customs.
2. **independent thinking**—To correlate relevant geographic data to draw logical answers.
3. **social responsibility**—How might people in other regions organize their societies to live better?
4. **democratic living**—Are the resources in other countries equally distributed?
5. **group cooperation**—Discuss how wastelands have been changed to valuable lands by cooperative efforts and modern technology such as irrigated desert areas.

Model Three

Social Science Area and Concept—Sociology and Political Science— Political representation is affected by and affects that country's social class system.

Specific Skills

1. To identify, factually, the various social economic classes in America and how they vote.
2. To explain the importance, difficulty, and effects of the checks and balances system.
3. To identify the basic parts of the constitution, how they are practiced in society, and mechanics for changing the constitution within the democratic process.

Attitudes Relevant to Topic

1. **empathy**—Political representation of the poor and ethnic minorities.
2. **independent thinking**—To base thoughts on studied evidence rather than just emotion.
3. **social responsibility**—Where is the greatest need for social and political reform in the various socioeconomic classes?

4. **democratic living**—Critical negative areas in our society.

5. **group cooperation**—Where is the most and least degree of socio-political cooperation found in our culture with accompanying reasons?

Model Four

Social Science Area and Concept—Economics and Political Science— A country's type of government greatly determines its economic life.

Specific Skills

1. To define and apply technical economic terms to contemporary economic problems.

2. The proper use of economic and political charts and graphs to interpret technical political-economic data.

3. To study the effects of lobbies on our economy with discussion of positive and negative effects.

Attitudes Relevant to Topics

1. **empathy**—Discuss the political and economic assets and liabilities of our welfare system.

2. **independent thinking**—To adapt correct terms and facts to revise preconceived biases.

3. **social responsibility**—What economic and political rules are vital for our nation's best interests?

4. **democratic living**—Are some groups treated unfairly in terms of both economic and political factors?

5. **group cooperation**—How can all citizens contribute to avoid mass inflation?

Bibliography

1. Zodikoff, David, "A Questionnaire Study of Social Attitudes of Intermediate Grade Children." *Research in Education,* December, 1970, U.S. Office of Education.

2. ———, "A Study of Social Attitudes of Intermediate Grade Children," *Research in Education,* January, 1971, U.S. Office of Education.

3. ———, "Suggested Models for Developing Social Studies Comprehension," *Research in Education,* February, 1971, U.S. Office of Education.

4. ———, "The Use of Comprehensive Models in Social Studies Instruction," *Research in Education,* February, 1972, U.S. Office of Education.

The comprehensive model is used in the following chapters because it encompasses the structural rationale of each of the other models. The key word in the model is interrelatedness that is done on a **deliberate** planning basis by the teacher before and during the actual teaching process. Therefore, the skills and content are so selected that they will aid the learner to develop those social attitudes related to the basic stated conceptual scheme.

A basic value of the comprehensive model is that it is open-ended enough that it can be utilized, structurally, with any standardized content-oriented text in grades kindergarten through twelve. This is true because the content selected is only the **means** to achieve a desired **goal** balancing attitudes, skills, and content within the desired conceptual theme. Obviously, this requires deliberate planning by the teacher before and during the presentation of the content.

CHAPTER 2

Concept Models
Related to Community Studies

INTRODUCTION

The basic organization in chapters II to IV will consist of the comprehensive model outline with briefly stated suggestions, questions, and classroom activities that should help increase both the teacher and student's use of the models. For the sake of further clarification, a uniform coding system will be used for each model in each chapter. The code has the following interpretation: the roman numeral refers to the chapter, S equals specific skills, with attached numbers referring to the skill mentioned in the model, and A equals the attitude areas with the same numbering scheme as used in the skills section. In the skills section, the numbered attitudes related to the skill should be expanded by teacher-made questions that would directly involve students in making decisions in each of the identified attitude areas.

Each chapter will have four separate comprehensive models and each model will have suggested classroom activities at both elementary and secondary school levels. A deliberate effort has been made to make each chapter's suggested content areas as broad as possible to allow for more flexibility of content choice. This helps to make content selection the means to achieve a balanced goal of uniting content learning with specific skill usage, and the inclusion of **conscious** efforts to develop the stated attitude areas, all related to a basic conceptual theme. The point should be made again that teachers and students continually try to find alternative structures to those found in the models.

In the classroom use of the comprehensive model approach, four basic problems must be met by the teacher **prior** to teaching the lessons in the unit. The first problem is to clearly define a conceptual theme toward which the specific skills, content, and attitudes will **directly** relate. A second problem is to select that content from one or more of the social sciences that **directly** relates to the understanding and development of the conceptual theme. The selection of **specific** subject skills needed by students directly relate to the understanding of the conceptual themes comprises the third problem area. The fourth task is to select those learning experiences that emphasize each of the five attitude areas so that students become actively involved with the discussion of these areas on a personal basis. A basic goal of the comprehensive model is to **interrelate** these various areas around the stated conceptual theme, to attempt to prevent the fragmented learning of concepts, skills, and attitudes.

The use of *Community Studies* to develop understanding of some of the problems of citizens in a democratic society.

COMPREHENSIVE MODEL OUTLINE ONE

Subject   Conceptual Theme

History: Past Events Cause Present Conditions in the Current Community.

Specific Skills

1. Evaluate early newspapers and documents to see what life was like in earlier times.
2. To practice judging reasons why some sources are more valid than others.
3. Construct sequential cause-effect time-line chart of local historical events.

Attitudes Relevant to Model

1. *social responsibility*—How do various agencies work to help us?
2. *independent thinking*—How may our community be improved for general well being?
3. *democratic living*—What new laws are needed to protect everyone's rights?
4. *empathy*—What people in the community do you feel sorry for and why?
5. *group cooperation*—How can citizens work together better to improve life for all?

Suggested Classroom Activities Related to Model

Classroom Activities

II (S1; A1, 2, 3, 4, 5) Have students read various news accounts of community interest in earlier and contempoary newspapers to see what similar and different community issues exist.

(S2; A1, 2) Using researched news items and various eye witness accounts, develop criteria for determining why some sources are more reliable than others in terms of degree of bias and presented evidence. .

(S3; A1, 2, 3, 4, 5) By development of a sequential cause-effect time-line chart, try to determine the origins of present community conditions, and reasons why present problems exist in the community, and what solutions are advisable for the total community.

COMPREHENSIVE MODEL OUTLINE TWO

Subject   Conceptual Theme

Geography: An Area's Physical Location Greatly Determines the Way People Live.

Specific Skills

1. Apply technical geographical terms to specifically locate and describe an area.
2. The use of basic map parts to draw general inferences of a given area.
3. By combined use of map skills and technical geographic terms relate why an area has its climate, topography, and ways of living.

Attitudes Relevant to Model

1. *social responsibility*—After learning present laws of community, how or why should some of the laws be changed?
2. *independent thinking*—To correlate relevant geographic data to draw logical answers.
3. *democratic living*—Consideration of how natural resources should be shared or distributed.
4. *empathy*—To identify with people of various customs.
5. *group cooperation*—Try to discover how various group efforts have helped to improve community life and what is still left to be done.

Suggested Activities Related to Model

(S1, 2, 3; A1, 2, 3, 4, 5) Use of national, state, and community maps to practice knowledge of key terms such as distortion, latitude, longitude, and the possible socioeconomic effects of physical location on the community's life styles. Also, compare and contrast the community with other world communities of varying contrasts. For example, in-depth studies of Arctic, Tropical, and Temperate communities, followed by written and oral reports explaining reasons for differences in food, clothing, shelter, social organization and other life style variables.

This type of activity is ideal for developing the attitude area of empathy, particularly by studying contrasting cultures and having students try to role-play how their values might change under varying physical, political and socioeconomic conditions.

COMPREHENSIVE MODEL OUTLINE THREE

Subject Areas   Conceptual Theme

Economics and Political Science: An Area's Economic Life and Government Structure Mutually Affect Each Other.

Specific Skills

1. To define and apply technical economic terms to contemporary economic problems.
2. To use economic and political charts and graphs to interpret technical political-economic data.
3. To study the effects of lobbies on our economy with discussion of positive and negative effects.

Attitudes Relevant to Topic

1. *social responsibility*—Try to determine what political-economic rules would be best for the entire community.
2. *independent thinking*—To encourage withholding opinions until actual data are studied.
3. *democratic living*—Discover which groups are most and least favored in the community and reasons.
4. *empathy*—What assets and problems exist in community relief and welfare systems?
5. *group cooperation*—What can each individual do to help avoid mass inflation?

Suggested Activities Related to Model

(S1; A1, 2, 3, 4, 5) By careful analysis of the meaning of such terms as gross-net income, money-real income, inflation-deflation, and others, reference and list examples from the economic life of the community to gain a realistic picture, and then list and discuss what political reforms are needed to help ensure a more stable economy and provide better standards of living.

(S2; A1, 2, 3, 4, 5) By use of published and student devised charts and graphs depicting economic and political data of community life, analyze and develop criteria related to needed reforms of those community groups with the poorest economic situation, and what political innovation could improve the problems.

(S3; A1, 2, 3, 4, 5) Determine, on the basis of evidence found in community newspapers, records, interviews, which lobbies or pressure groups are most successful in a community to their own interest groups, and to what extent the lobbies help or hinder the general good of the community, and what political or legal devices can be utilized to ensure the good of the community.

COMPREHENSIVE MODEL OUTLINE FOUR

Subject Areas   Conceptual Theme

Sociology and Political Science: Political Representation Is Affected by and Affects the Community's Social Class system

Specific Skills

1. To identify, factually, the various socioeconomic classes in the areas and how they vote.

2. Determine the extent of success of an equitable political check-balance system.

3. How the Federal Constitution affects the social and political life of the community and the legal mechanical means for change.

Attitudes Relevant to Topic

1. *social responsibility*—To decide where greatest needs lie to reform the sociopolitical realities of a given community.

2. *independent thinking*—To attempt to differ between the judgments based on emotions rather than from studied evidence.
3. *democratic living*—Most critical negative social areas, and political means of improvement.
4. *empathy*—Political representation of economically poor and ethnic minorities in the community.
5. *group cooperation*—Where the most and least degree of sociopolitical cooperation is found in an area including relevant reasons.

Suggested Activities Related to the Model

II (S1; A1, 2, 3, 4, 5) By use of community maps, and other written materials, determine the political voting structure of various socioeconomic groups in the community. By inference, determine reasons for political choice and to what extent the various socioeconomic classes have been helped or hindered by their elected choice.

(S2; A2, 3, 4, 5) After a detailed study of the mechanics of a political tripartite checks and balances system, use charts and discussion sessions to evaluate the postive and negative effects on both a local and national level.

(S3; A1, 2, 3, 4, 5) After an extensive study of the federal constitution, develop student involvement in written lists and/or essays, including on-going discussions pertaining to how the Constitution might be amended to ensure greater cooperation between various social and political groups.

Additional Classroom Activities for Chapters II to IV

Students are encouraged to expand on the skills, attitudes and activities already mentioned in the chapter and to seek newer structures within the models. Also, when developing any of the models, strive to follow the operational definitions of the social attitudes when seeking to select content relevant to the model.

Chapter III— North America (Repeat Model 2 structure of Chapter II)

Chapter IV—A Comparative Study of an Asiatic and African Country (Same Model structure as Chapters II and III)

CHAPTER 3

A Study of North America

COMPREHENSIVE MODEL OUTLINE FIVE

Subject   Conceptual Theme

History: Certain Events in History Can Drastically Change a Country's Present and Future Development.

Specific Skills

1. Analysis of primary and secondary source documents to ascertain actual past happenings.
2. Developing a sequential time-line chart to aid in conceptualizing cause-effect relations.
3. Write short reports analyzing past events and persons based on evaluation of original and secondary sources.

Attitudes Relevant to Topic

1. *social responsibility*—By careful study of the Federal Constitution, determine to what extent the rights and responsibilities of American citizens, past and present, are being practiced.
2. *independent thinking*—Analysis of original sources to determine the accuracy and dependability of their content.
3. *democratic living*—A chronological sequentially developed study of American society to see what evidence there is that the respect for the rights of others has been developed since earlier times.
4. *empathy*—The identification of minority groups in past and present American society, and how they were treated during each period.
5. *group cooperation*—A continuous study of the successes and failures of various groups in American history in achieving their particular goals.

Suggested Classroom Activities Related to Topic

Classroom Activities

(S1; A1, 2, 3, 4, 5) By continuous analysis of original sources related to major events such as the causes and effects of the Revolutionary and Civil War, develop questions which would involve direct student use of the five attitude areas.

(**Example**—Was the treatment of American Indians changed after the Revolutionary War, if not, what were the reasons?)

(S2; A2, 3, 5) List major events of the colonial, early national and post-civil war periods to ascertain causal relationships in history.

(S3; A1, 2, 3, 4, 5) Have students write short interpretive essays of specific past events or personalities stressing the use of original sources, in order to differentiate fact from fiction and the ideal from the real.

COMPREHENSION MODEL OUTLINE SIX

Subject   Conceptual Theme

Geography: Man and His Physical Environment Are Interdependent.

Specific Skills

1. To read, construct, and interpret various types of maps.
2. To define and apply technical geographical terms in order to expand geographical concepts.
3. To differentiate physical and social or man-made data to help in determining interdependent factors.

Attitudes Relevant to Topic

1. *social responsibility*—To what extent have man-made rules or laws helped him to adapt to his environment?
2. *independent thinking*—To what extent has man learned to control his environment, and in what areas is man still vulnerable to natural factors?
3. *democratic living*—In past and present North American societies has there been evidence of the sharing of the land's area and

natural resources, and what more, if any, should be done to improve in this area?

4. *empathy*—To what extent should the natural wealth of land and resources be shared amongst the total population?

5. *group cooperation*—What past and present evidence is there to illustrate the role of human technology to improve and/or deplete the natural phenomena of North America?

Suggested Classroom Activities Related to Topic

Classroom Activities

(S1; A1, 2, 5) By the study and construction of various types of maps such as population, relief, topographical, climate, students should develop inferences, based on data observation, explaining reasons for heavy and light population centers and ways of livelihood as a direct result of various environmental factors.

(S2; A1, 2, 3) To define and apply technical geographical terms as they apply to explain various modes of living and livelihood in different parts of North America.

(S3; A1, 2, 3, 4, 5) List and explain the accomplishments of science that aided man to cope with his natural surroundings, as well as listing and explaining how man is still very vulnerable to extreme natural phenomena (e.g., hurricanes, earthquakes, drought, and others).

COMPREHENSIVE MODEL OUTLINE SEVEN

Subject Areas   Conceptual Theme

Economics and Political Science: The Political and Economic Systems of North America Are Mutually Interdependent.

Specific Skills

1. To identify the various units of the Federal government and what direct and indirect roles they play in affecting the nation's economy.

2. To recognize the role and political-economic effects of lobbies on both the Federal and State levels.

3. To define the process of Federal and State tax systems and inter-relate with the expenditures of Federal and State budget plans.

Attitudes Relevant to Topic

1. *social responsibility*—Should and how can present tax laws be reformed in order to achieve more equity between various socio-economic classes?

2. *independent thinking*—What specific changes should be made in our present government to ensure more improved reforms of our economic policies?

3. *democratic living*—Should citizens that pay higher taxes have more voting power than those that pay less taxes?

4. *empathy*—Has the government done too much or too little in giving economic help to underpriviliged people in our country? If so, what should they do now?

5. *group cooperation*—What political reforms are necessary to prevent massive inflationary spirals?

Suggested Classroom Activities Related to Topic

Classroom Activities

(S1; A1, 2, 3, 4, 5) By the use of almanacs and statistical year-books, chart the various departments and bureaus of the Federal government with a brief explanation of each agency's role in affecting the economy. (e.g., Department of Health, Education, and Welfare is directly involved with expenditures for public health, education, and welfare.

(S2; A1, 2, 3, 4, 5) Use relevant resource materials to identify major lobby or private interest groups, their influence on the law-making process and the National and State economy.

(S3; A1, 2, 3, 4, 5) After a study of Federal and State tax forms, examine the budget items of each level to determine the sources and expenditures of tax revenues, including suggestions for positive reforms.

COMPREHENSIVE MODEL OUTLINE EIGHT

Subject Areas   Conceptual Theme

Sociology and Political Science: The Political and Social-Class Structures of North America Directly Affect Each Other.

Specific Skills

1. To recognize voting trends, by use of the Congressional Record, to determine the influences of sectional interests on Federal legislation.

2. To identify and explain the desired political objectives of various ethnic and economic groups in North America.

3. To list the various socioeconomic classes in North America and try to explain how their attitudes are expressed in the State and Federal political levels.

Attitudes Relevant to Topic

1. *social responsibility*—To what extent are the rights and duties of American citizens being practiced or violated in contemporary life?

2. *independent thinking*—What political reforms are necessary today, on both the State and Federal levels, to help ensure a more balanced economy?

3. *democratic living*—Are any political and/or legal reforms necessary to balance the representative power of ethnic minorities and lower socioeconomic groups?

4. *empathy*—What ethnic and economic groups in America today are in the greatest need of social and political change?

5. *group cooperation*—How and why do lobbies and other special interest groups succeed in helping to get favorable new legislation?,

Suggested Classroom Activities Related to Topic

Classroom Activities

(S1; A1, 2, 3, 4, 5) By the use of basic reference sources such as the Congressional Record, statistical yearbooks and others, prepare oral and written reports depicting the influences of sectional interests on Federal and State legislation.

(S2; A1, 2, 3, 4, 5) Read and interpret the various social, educational, and economic goals of various ethnic minorities and prepare reports explaining which goals are justified, reasonable, or unrealistic and unattainable.

(S3; A1, 2, 3, 4, 5) By the use of statistical yearbooks, and almanacs, identify the various socioeconomic levels in America today; use this data with present income tax laws to determine which of these socioeconomic classes are in the greatest need for political, social, and economic reform.

CHAPTER 4

A Study of Asia and Africa .

COMPREHENSIVE MODEL OUTLINE NINE

Subject   Conceptual Theme

History: Major Events in The History of a Nation Affects Its Present and Future Conditions.

Specific Skills

1. Locate and read primary source accounts depicting major social, economic, political, and cultural changes in Asian and African history.

2. Investigate and determine the effects of thoughts and actions of past and present Asian and African leaders in relation to vital changes in Asian and African cultures.

3. Develop a sequential cause-effect chronology chart of Asia and Africa including specific interrelationships between key events and individuals or groups.

Attitudes Relevant to Topic

1. *social responsibility*—What legal changes have occurred in Africa between older tribal customs and newer political types, and what countries in Asia, China for example, have drastically changed the people's role in legislative processes?

2. *independent thinking*—Have modern social and economic developments improved the living standards of Asia's and Africa's peoples?

3. *democratic living*—Are more freedoms and political voice found today in most of Asia and Africa when compared with earlier cultures?

4. *empathy*—What noticeable improvements, if any, in basic individual rights can be found in Asia and Africa today compared to life in earlier times?

5. *group cooperation*—Why were some revolutionary groups in Asia and Africa more successful in gaining political power than others?

Suggested Classroom Activities Related to Topic

Classroom Activities

(S1, A1, 2, 3, 4, 5) Read various primary and secondary source accounts of past Asian and African cultures written by Asian, African, and western writers and try to determine what cultural biases exist in different authors.

(S2; A1, 2, 3, 4, 5) By the careful study of autobiographies, biographies, and other sources, try to determine what Asian and African leaders were actually like by comparing statements about these leaders by themselves, their friends, and enemies.

(S3; A1, 2, 3, 4, 5) At each stage of writing a sequential chronology chart of major events, be able to explain why these events were included in the chart in terms of the effects of these particular events on the future life of the countries.

COMPREHENSIVE MODEL OUTLINE TEN

Subject   Conceptual Theme

Geography: The Physical and Climatic Features of Asia and Africa Directly Influence The People's Manner of Living.

Specific Skills

1. Develop the ability to interpret and construct various types of maps, such as physical, political, population, to broaden conceptual understandings related to varying life styles in Asia and Africa.

2. Define and apply technical geographical concepts as they apply to the geographic data of Asia and Africa.

3. Organize and write brief research essays comparing and contrasting various life styles in Asia and Africa, including reasons for such differences based on differences in climate, location, and topography.

Attitudes Relevant to Topic

1. *social responsibility*—What types of political systems are found in Asia and Africa, and why are some types more prevalent than others?

2. *independent thinking*—What particular social, economic, and political problems are found in new emerging Asian and African countries that are not found in more modern established countries, and what reasons account for these problems?

3. *democratic living*—To what extent is the natural wealth of Asia and Africa shared with its people, and what changes should be made to improve conditions?

4. *empathy*—What obvious reforms are necessary in various societies of Asia and Africa to improve the social, political, and cultural levels of its peoples?

5. *group cooperation*—What evidence of the presence or lack of close cooperation within various Asian and African cultures helps to explain their development or retarded growth?

Suggested Classroom Activities Related to Topic

Classroom Activities

(S1; A1, 2, 5) Have separate groups of students each do a specific map of Asia and Africa. For example, one group depict topographical data, another climatic, population, industrial, and agricultural; after each group completes one area, provide each student with the various maps and their data so they will be able to conceptualize more broadly by tying isolated facts together.

(S2; A1, 2, 3, 4, 5) Have students write reports, including the correct use of technical geographic terms, on various Asian and African cultures, and/or comparative studies of an African with an Asian culture.

(S3; A1, 2, 3, 4, 5) Combined with S2, have comparative charts made and outlined depicting the various climatic and topographical regions of Asia and Africa, including their effects on the cultural, economic, and social life styles of the people.

COMPREHENSIVE MODEL OUTLINE ELEVEN

Subject Areas　　　　　　　　Conceptual Theme

Economics and Political Science: A Country's Type of Government Directly Affects Its Economic Way of Life.

Specific Skills

1. By the use of almanacs, statistical yearbooks, and economic and political texts, interpret and construct economic tables and graphs accompanied by inferences related to political causes for such economic facts.

2. By source readings and use of standard reference works, identify various types of political governments in Asia and Africa, relate with their economic system, and explain possible differences.

3. Compare and contrast the political and economic system of the United States with that of various Asian and African countries, carefully stirring to separate fact from opinion.

Attitudes Relevant to Topic

1. *social responsibility*—To what extent do the various types of political structures found in Asian and African countries help or hinder the economic stability of these countries?

2. *independent thinking*—Which countries in Asia and Africa are the most economically depressed, and to what extent is the political system of these countries to blame for such conditions?

3. *democratic living*—Find evidence to show in which Asian and African countries is found considerable suppression of individual rights, defending or criticizing such facts in terms of economic, geographic, and historical data.

4. *empathy*—In terms of greater sharing of economic wealth and more individual political freedoms, which countries in Asia and Africa are in the greatest need of reform?

5. *group cooperation*—From a comparative approach, which Asian and African countries have the more efficient economic and political systems, based in part on evidenced close cooperation between the government and the people?(Examples relevant to this question would be presence or absence of revolutionary groups, labor strikes, and frequency of changes in political offices.)

Suggested Classroom Activities Related to Topic

Classroom Activities

(S1; A1, 2, 5) Have students construct graphs and charts depicting the various political structures and functions, and economic data, and present summaries in the form of mock debates, model governments, written essays, or oral individual reports.

(S2; A1, 2, 3, 4, 5) Combined with S1, have student groups role-play various political types and defend their particular structures citing economic and social realities.

(S3; A1, 2, 3, 4, 5) Divide class into various groups so that each group can research and then present oral arguments to the entire class why their particular political and economic systems are more effective than others.

(Example—a pro-U.S. and anti-U.S. group and a pro-Rhodesia and pro-Chinese Republic group.)

COMPREHENSIVE MODEL OUTLINE TWELVE

Subject Areas   Conceptual Theme

Sociology and Political Science: The Various Social Conditions Found in Asia and Africa Are Directly Related to Various Types of Political Systems.

Specific Skills

1. To identify technical terms peculiar to Sociology and Political Science, and to give relevant examples using these terms to describe the social and political systems found in Africa and Asia.
2. To describe the various social classes in Asia and Africa, and explain their political roles.
3. To compare and contrast the various political systems found in Asia and Africa, and to determine the historical, social, geographic and economic reasons for the existence of these various political systems.

Attitudes Relevant to Topic

1. *social responsibility*—In which of the political systems in Asia and Africa do citizens have a greater role in the law-making processes?

2. *independent thinking*—In which political systems is there found the greatest gap between goveing groups and the citizens, and why is this so?

3. *democratic living*—Is there evidence that wealthier social classes in various Asian and African countries have more political power than poorer classes, and if so, what reforms should be instituted?

4. *empathy*—Describe what you think your life would be like if you were a citizen in some Asian or African country. Compare and contrast this life with the one you're living now as an American citizen.

5. *group cooperation*—Which Asian and African countries seem to have the most and least amount of conflict between the ruling class and the various social classes, and what reasons are there for this amount or lack of cooperation between these various groups?

Suggested Classroom Activities Related to Topic

Classroom Activities

(S1; A1, 2, 3, 4, 5) Have students write comparative reports of varying Asian and African countries, listing the folkways, mores, and other technical terms to give evidence that they understand the meaning and use of these terms.

(S2; A1, 2, 3, 4, 5) By the use of written essays or panel reports, research and present to the class reports of the various social classes found the amount of political power found in each.

(S3; A1, 2, 3, 4, 5) In order to encourage the use of a broad fields or total culture approach in the study of an area, suggest that students, in their research, isolate political, social, economic, historical, and geographic factors first, and then synthesize these various areas to broaden their conceptualization of a given country.

APPENDIX 1

World and Continent Maps

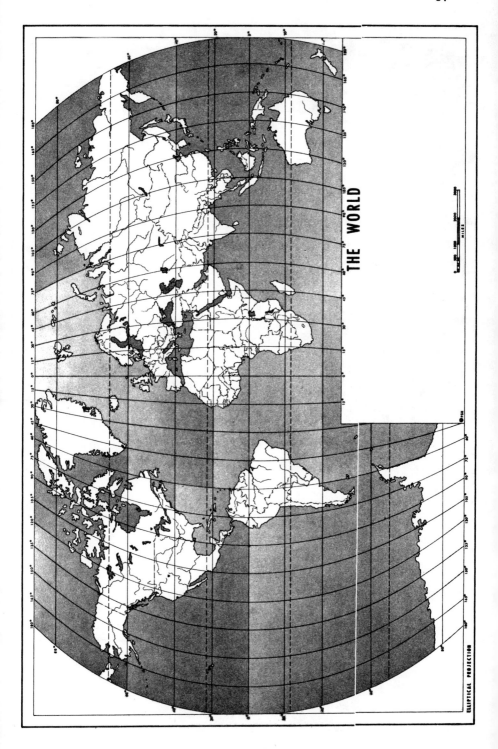

THE WORLD

ELLIPTICAL PROJECTION

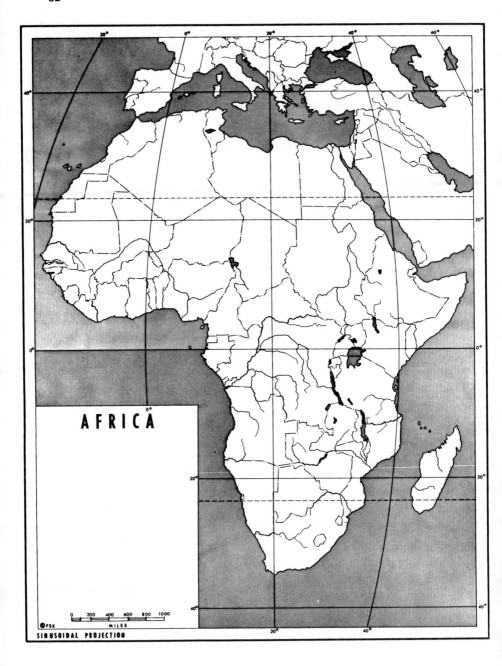

AFRICA

0 200 400 600 800 1000

MILES

PSK

SINUSOIDAL PROJECTION

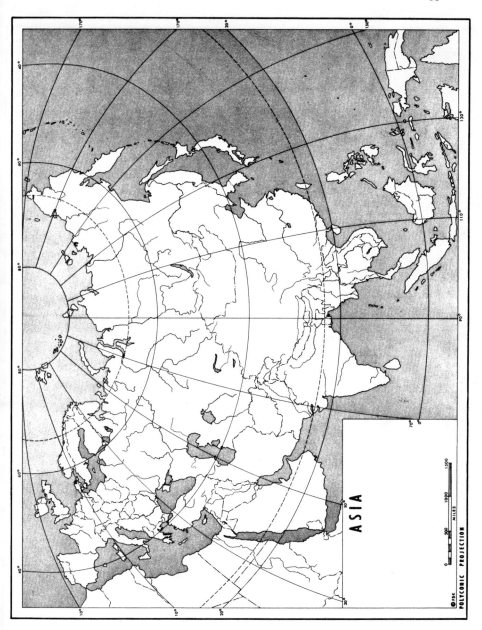

ASIA

POLYCONIC PROJECTION

MILES
0   500   1000   1500

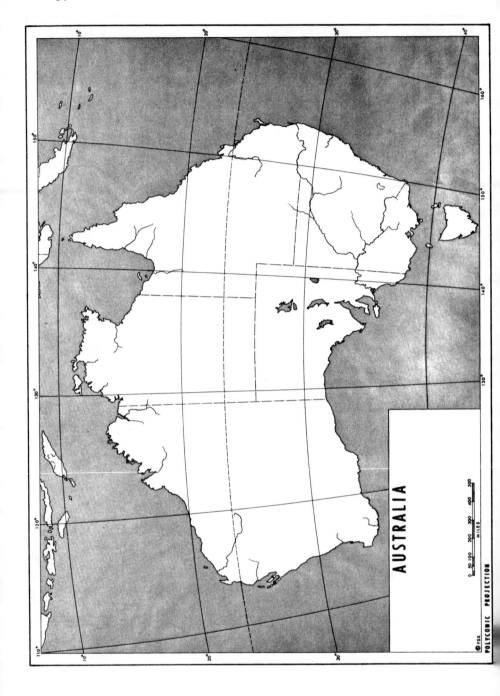

AUSTRALIA

0 50 100 200 300 400 500
MILES

© FBK

POLYCONIC PROJECTION

55

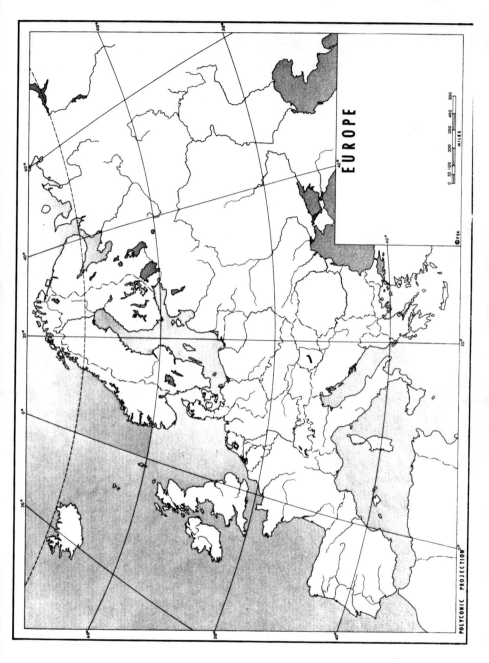

EUROPE

POLYCONIC PROJECTION

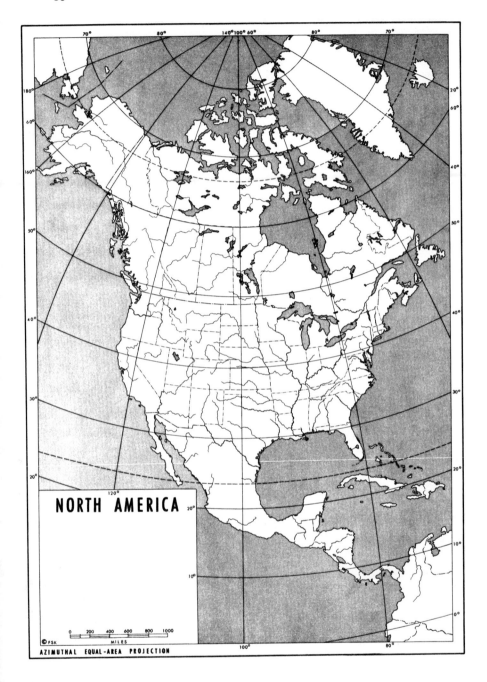

NORTH AMERICA

0   200   400   600   800   1000
MILES
© FSK
AZIMUTHAL EQUAL-AREA PROJECTION

SOUTH AMERICA

SINUSOIDAL PROJECTION

0   200   400   600   800   1000
© FSK   MILES

Antarctic

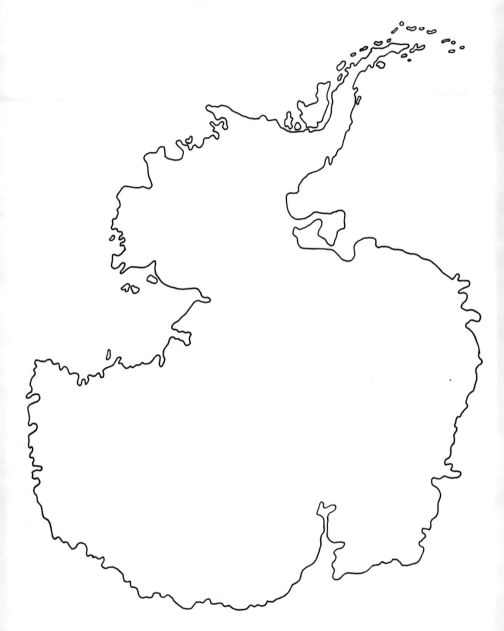

APPENDIX 2

Statistics of Selected World Countries

CHILE

Area: 292,256 sq. mi.; Population: 8,834,820 (1970 census).

Official Name: Republic of Chile; Capital: Santiago; Nationality: Chilean; Languages: The official and virtually universal language is Spanish; Religion: Overwhelmingly Roman Catholic;
Flag: A white horizontal stripe over a longer red stripe, with a blue
square in the upper left corner containing a 5-pointed white star;
Anthem: National Song, beginning "Pure Chile, thy skies spread
above thee"; Currency: Escudo (12.33 per U.S. $1).

Location: Southwest coast of South America. Chile is bordered on
the north by Peru, on the east by Argentina and Boliva, on the south
by Drake Passage, and on the west by the Pacific Ocean; Features: The country sketches some 2,650 miles along the Pacific
coast and is at no point wider than 250 miles. The north is desert,
the central region argicultural, and the south is forest land. The
towering Andes dominate most of the eastern frontier; Chief
Rivers: Loa, Maule, Bio-Bio, Valdiva.

Head of State and of Government: President Salvador Allende, born
1909, elected by Congress in October 1970; Effective Date of Present Constitution: 1925; Legislative Body: Congress (bicameral),
consisting of the Senate and the Chamber of Deputies. The Senate
has 50 members elected by direct popular vote for 8 years. The
Chamber of Deputies has 150 members elected by popular vote for 4
years; Local Government: 25 provinces, each headed by an inten-
dant.

Ethnic Composition: About 68% of the population is of Spanish-
Indian descent, 30% of European (mainly Spanish) descent, and 2%
Indian; Population Distribution: 74% urban; Density: 33 inhabi-
tants per sq. mi.

Largest Cities: (1970 census) Santiago 2,586,212, Valparaiso
292,847 Concepcion 196,317, Vina del Mar 153,085, Antofagasta
137,968.

Per Capita Income: $674 (1969 est.); Gross National Product
(GNP): $6.1 billion (1969 est.); Economic Statistics: 18% of GNP is
derived from industry (paper and paper products, iron and steel,
petrochemicals, chemicals, and metal products); 14% from commerce: 11% from mining; 7% for services, and 4.5% from agriculture

(wheat, wine grapes, potatoes, sugar beets, tobacco, fruit); **Minerals and Mining:** Chile is one of the world's leading copper producers. iron ore is second in importance; natural nitrates, petroleum, manganese, lead, and zinc are also exploited; **Labor Force:** About 2.75 million; about 27% in services, 25% in agriculture, 19% in manufacturing, and 14% in commerce; **Foreign Trade:** Exports, mainly copper and copper manufactures, iron ore, pulp and paper, fishmeal, wool, and fruit, totaled $1 billion in 1969. Imports, mainly machinery and equipment, agricultural products, and transport equipment, totaled $907 million. **Principal Trade Partners:** United States, Latin American Free Trade Association, West Germany, Britain, the Netherlands, Japan.

Vital Statistics: Birthrate: 29.2 per 1,000 of pop.; death rate, 9; **Life Expectancy:** 62 years; **Health Statistics:** 250 inhabitants per hospital bed; 1,790 per physician; **Infant Mortality:** 83.4 per 1,000 births; **Illiteracy:** 11% **Education Statistics:** 8,692 primary and secondary schools, with combined enrollment of 2,387,000; **Enrollment in Higher Education:** 82,000 (1970); **GNP Expended on Education:** 3.9% (1966).

Transportation: Surface roads total 4,446 mi.; **Motor Vehicles:** 285,441 (1969); **Passenger Cars:** 1,700,000 (1967); **Railway Mileage:** 5,943; **Ports:** Valparaiso, Africa, Antofagasta, Punta Arenas; **Major Airlines:** LAN-Chile, the government-owned airline, operates domestic and international services; **Communications:** Largely privately owned; **Radio Stations:** 218; **Receivers:** 2,500,000 (1970); **Television Stations:** 12; **Receivers:** 200,000 (1969) **Telephones:** 334,415 (1969); **Newspapers:** 46 dailies, 118 copies per 1,000 inhabitants.

Weights and Measures: Metric system; **Travel Requirements:** (1971) Passport, tourist card (obtainable on arrival) valid for 3 months, no fee.

UNITED STATES

Area: 3,617,204 sq. mi.; **Population:** 203,184,772 (1970 census). **Official Name:** United States of America; **Capital:** Washington, D.C.; **Nationality:** American or United States; **Languages:** English is the official and predominant language. Spanish is the preferred language of sizeable minorities in New York City (chiefly Puerto Rican migrants), Florida (Cuban refugees), and along the Mexican border. Other minority languages include Italian, German, Polish, Yiddish, Russian, American Indian tongues, Chinese, and Japanese; **Religion:** About two thirds of the population is Protestant, one fourth Roman Catholic, 3% Jewish, and the rest of other or no affiliation; **Flag:** Popularly known as the "Stars and Stripes" or "Old Glory," the flag consists of 13 horizontal alternate red and white stripes, and a union of 50 five-pointed white stars arranged in alternate rows of 6 and of 5 on a blue field in the upper left corner; **Anthem:** The Star-Spangled Banner.

Location: The United States proper (excluding Hawaii and Alaska) stretches across North America from the Atlantic Ocean on the east to the Pacific Ocean on the west, from Canada on the north to Mexico, the Gulf of Mexico, and the Gulf of California on the south; **Features:** The United States proper (excluding Hawaii and Alaska) consists of the Atlantic coastal plain, the Appalachian highlands, a vast interior plains region, the Rocky Mountains belt, the intermontane basin and plateaus west of the Rockies, and the mountains and valleys of the Pacific borderland. Another division, part of the Laurentian Plain of Canada, dips into the United States in the Great Lakes region. Alaska's main physical divisions are the Pacific mountain system, the Central Plateau, the Arctic mountain system, and the Arctic Slope. Hawaii consists of a 1,610-mile-long chain of 122 islands, which represent the peaks of a chain of mountains of volcanic origin and largely submerged in the Pacific; **Chief Rivers:** Mississippi, Missouri, Rio Grande, Yukon, Arkansas, Colorado, Ohio-Allegheny, Red, Columbia.

Head of State and Government: President Richard M. Nixon, born 1913, elected 1968; **Effective Date of Constitution:** March 4, 1789; **Legislative Body:** Congress (bicameral), consisting of the Senate and the House of Representatives. The Senate consists of 100 members—2 from each state—chosen by popular vote for a 6-year term; a third of its membership is renewed every 2 years. The House of Representatives has 435 members elected by popular vote every 2 years; each state is entitled to at least one Representative, with the total number determined periodically according to population; **Local Government:** 50 states, each with a popularly elected governor and legislature. Below the state level, local self-government is usually conducted through municipalities, townships, and counties.

Ethnic Composition: The nation's ethnic diversity is chiefly due to large-scale immigration, most of which took place before 1920. Whites comprise about 88% of the population, Negroes 11%, and other races the remaining 1%; **Population Distribution:** 73.5% urban, 26.5% rural; **Density:** 57.4 inhabitants per sq. mi.

Largest Cities (M.A. = Metropolitan Area): 1970 census New York 7,868,000 M.A. 11,529,000; Chicago 3,367,000. M.A. 6,979,000; Los Angeles 2,816,000. M.A. 7,032,000; Philadelphia 1,949,000. M.A. 4,818,000; Detroit 1,511,000. M.A. 4,200,000; Houston 1,233,000. M.A. 1,985,000; Baltimore 906,000. M.A. 2,071,000; Dallas 844,000. M.A. 1,556,000; Washington, D.C. 757,000. M.A. 2,861,000; Cleveland 751,000. M.A. 2,064,000.

Per Capita Income: $3,910 (1970); **Gross National Product (GNP):** $976.5 billion (1970 estimate); **Economic Statistics:** About 27% of the GNP is derived from manufacturing; 16% from wholesale and retail trade; 15% from finance, insurance, and real estate; 11% from services; 10% from government and government enterprises; 6% from agriculture, forestry, and fisheries; 5% from construction; 4% each from transportation and communications, electric, gas, and sanitary services; 2% from mining and other sources; **Minerals and Mining:** The United States produces more minerals and uses more than any other nation in the world. It is the world's leading producer of oil (about one-fourth of world output) and of copper, and ranks second to the Soviet Union in production of coal and iron ore. It produces more than 60% of the world output of natural gas, and between 70% and 80% of world output of mica, agricultural nitrogen, and molybdenum. Zinc, lead, sulfur, vanadium, cadmium, uranium, phosphate rock, bauxite, fluorspar, nitrates, quicksilver, potash, limestone, cement rock, borates, gold, and silver are among the other major minerals produced, and the nation is also rich in waterpower; **Labor Force:** 85.7 million, of which more than 95% is engaged in nonagricultural industries. The average factory worker earns about $150 a week; **Foreign Trade**: Exports, chiefly machinery and transport equipment, food and live animals, crude materials (soybeans, textile fibers, ores and metal scrap), chemicals, other manufactured goods (metals and manufactures, scientific instruments, textiles, rubber, and paper), and mineral fuels, totaled $36.5 billion in 1969. Imports, mainly machinery and transport equipment, other manufactured goods (metals and manufactures, textiles, iron and steel-mill products, and nonferrous base metals), food and live animals, crude materials, and mineral fuels, totaled $35.8 billion; **Principal Trade Partners**: ,Canada, Japan, Britain, West Germany, Netherlands, Mexico, Italy, France.

Vital Statistics: Birthrate, 18.2 per 1,000 of pop.; death rate, 9.4; **Life Expectancy**: 70.2 years; **Health Statistics**: 122.4 inhabitants per hospital bed; 596.7 per physician; **Infant Mortality**: 19.8 per 1,000 births; **Illiteracy**: 1%; **Education Statistics**: 117,190 primary and secondary schools, with combined enrollment of 51,391,000 pupils; **Enrollment in Higher Education**: 8,498,117; **GNP Expended on Education**: 7.7%.

Transportation: Surfaced roads total 2,939,898 mi.; **Motor Vehicles**: 108,977,000 (1970); **Passengers Cars**: 89,861,000 (1970); **Railway Mileage**: 207,005; **Ports**: New York, Philadelphia, Portland, Baltimore, Boston, Mobile, Baton Rouge, San Francisco, New Orleans, Los Angeles; **Major Airlines**: Major international and domestic carriers are American Airlines, Braniff Airways, Eastern Airlines, Trans World Airlines, Pan American World Airways, Continental Air Lines, Delta Airlines, National Airlines, Northwest Orient Airlines, and United Airlines; **Communications**: Privately owned; **Radio Stations**: 4,636; **Receivers**: 285,000,000; **Television Stations**: 673; **Receivers**: 81,000,000; **Telephones**: 120,000,000; **Newspapers**: 1,748 dailies, 304.8 per 1,000 inhabitants.

Weights and Meausres: Avoirdupois units of weight and linear measures.

JAPAN

Area: 142,812 sq. mi.; Population: 103.7 million (1970 est.).

Official Name: Japan; Capital: Tokyo; Nationality: Japanese; Languages: Japanese is the official and universal language; Religion: Buddhism and Shintoism are the chief religions; virtually all Japanese practice one or the other and many subscribe to both; Flag: A red sun on a white field; Anthem: The Reign of Our Emperor; Currency: Yen (357 per U.S. $1).

Location: Japan is an archipelago forming a 2,000-mile-long arc off the east coast of Asia, between the Sea of Japan and the Pacific Ocean proper. It consists of four main islands: Hokkaido, Honshu, Shikoku, and Kyushu, and more than 3,000 smaller islands; Features: About four-fifths of the country is covered by hills and mountains, many of them active or dormant volcanoes. Because of the country's unstable geological position beside the Pacific deeps, numerous earthquakes are felt throughout the islands; Chief Rivers: Tone, Shinano, Ishikari, Kitakami.

Head of State: Emperor Hirohito, born 1901, ascended the throne 1926; Head of Government: Prime Minister Eisaku Sato, born 1901, elected by parliament in 1964; Effective Date of Present Constitution: May 3, 1947; Legislative Body: Parliament, or Diet (bicameral), consisting of the House of Representatives and the House of Councillors. The House of Representatives has 486 members elected for 4 years, plus 5 members for the Ryuku Islands. The House of Councillors has 250 members elected for 6 years, plus 2 members elected from the Ryuku Islands; Local Government: 46 prefectures, each with an elected mayor of governor and local assembly.

Ethnic Composition: The Japanese are a Mongoloid people, closely related to the other groups of east Asia, although there is evidence of admixture with Malayan and Caucasoid strains. Some 600,000 Koreans constitute the only important minority group; about 15,000 Ainu in Hokkaido, who are physically similar to Caucasians, are rapidly being assimilated; Population Distribution: 68% urban; Density: 725 inhabitants per sq. mi.

Largest Cities: (1970 estimates) Tokyo 8,840,942, Osaka 2,980,487, Yokohama 2,238,264, Nagoya 2,036,053, Kyoto 1,419,165, Kobe 1,288,937, Kitakyushu 1,042,321.

Per Capita Income: $1,289 (1969); Gross National Product (GNP): $165.8 billion (1969); Economic Statistics: 36.8% of GNP comes from industry (transportation equipment, electrical machinery, iron and steel, chemicals); 8.1% from agriculture (rice, vegetables, fruit, wheat, barley, and potatoes); 23.1% from trade; 11.1% from services; Minerals and Mining: Coal is plentiful but only about 25% can be used for industrial purposes. There are small amounts of copper, zinc, aluminum, lead, and nickel; Labor Force: 51,530,000 (1970), with 26.7% employed in industry, 16.3% in agriculture, and 14.6% in services; Foreign Trade: Exports, cheifly iron and steel, textiles, electronic equipment, motor vehicles, ships, totaled $19.31 billion in 1970. Imports, chiefly mineral fuels, metal ores and scrap, machinery and equipment, and foodstuffs, totaled $18.88 billion; Principal Trade Partners: United States, Australia, Canada, Iran, West Germany.

Vital Statistics: Birthrate, 18.6 per 1,000 of population; death rate, 7; Life Expectancy: 71 years; Health Statistics: 83 inhabitants per hospital bed; 898 per physician; Infant Mortality: 14.2 per 1,000 births; Illiteracy: 1-2%; Education Statistics: 42,359 primary and secondary schools, with combined enrollment of 18,706,198 pupils; Enrollment in Higher Education: 1,659,826; GNP Expended on Education: 12.5%.

Transportation: Surfaced roads total 77,312 mi.; Motor Vehicles: 16,528,521 (1970); Passenger Cars: 7,270,573 (1970); Railway Mileage: 15,728 mi.; Ports: Yokohama, Kobe, Tokyo, Nagoya Osaka, Yokkaichi; Major Airlines: Japan Air Lines, partly government owned and partly privately financed, operates international and domestic flights; Communications: Both government and privately owned; Radio Stations: 769; Receivers: 26 million; Television Stations: 168; Receivers: 22.7 million; Telephones: 19,899,000; Newspapers: 169 dailies, 503 copies per 1,000 inhabitants.

Weights and Measures: Metric system; Travel Requirements: (1971) Passport, multiple-entry visa valid for 4 years from date of issue for stay up to 60 days, no fee, onward ticket; traveler should consult the nearest consulate for other requirements depending on the kind of visa, and vaccination information.

CANADA

Area: 3,851,809 sq. mi.; **Population:** 21,400,000 (1970 est).

Official Name: Canada; **Capital:** Ottawa; **Nationality:** Canadian; **Languages:** English and French are both official languages, but only about 12% of the population is bilingual; 80% speaks English, 31% French, and 1% other languages such as German, Ukrainian, and Italian; **Religion:** 48% Roman Catholic; 20% United Church of Canada—a union of Presbyterians, Methodists, and Congregationalists; and 13% Anglican. The rest is made up of Presbyterians, Lutherans, Baptists, and Jews; **Flag:** A narrow, vertical red stripe on either side of a broad white field containing a red maple leaf; **Anthem:** O Canada (unofficial); God Save the Queen (royal anthem); **Currency:** Dollar (1.01 per U.S. $1).

Location: North America, occupying all of the continent north of the United States except for Alaska and the French islands of St. Pierre and Miquelon, both in the Gulf of St. Lawrence. The second largest country in the world, Canada is bordered on the north by the Arctic Ocean; on the east by Baffin Bay, the Davis Strait, and the Atlantic Ocean; on the south by the United States; and on the west by the Pacific Ocean and Alaska; **Features:** The Shield, a rugged area of pre-Cambrian rock, covers most of eastern and central Canada, or roughly half the entire country. To the north is the Arctic Archipelago and to the west of the Shield is a vast prairie region stretching to the Canadian Rockies, Westernmost Canada, which comprises most of British Columbia, is laced Canadian Rockies, Westernmost Canada, which comprises most of British Columbia, is laced Columbia, Churchill.

Head of State: Queen Elizabeth II, represented by a governor-general, Daniel Roland Michener, born 1900, appointed 1967; **Head of Government:** Prime Minister Pierre Elliott Trudeau, born 1921, appointed 1968; **Effective Date of Present Constitution:** The British North America Act of 1867 provides Canada with a form of written constitution; however, as in Britain, many of the country's legal and parliamentary practices are based on unwritten conventions; **Legislative Body:** Parliament (bicameral), consisting of a Senate and a House of Commons. The Senate consists of a maximum of 102 members, appointed until age 75 by the governor general on the advice of the prime minister. The House of Commons has 264 members, elected for 5 years; **Local Government:** 10 provinces, governed by a premier and an elected legislature. There are also 2 large northern territories—Yukon and the Northwest Territories. Yukon is governed by a federal government commissioner and a council of 7 elected members. The Northwest Territories are governed by a commissioner and a council of 9—of whom 5 are appointed and 4 elected.

Ethnic Composition: About 44% of the population is of British descent and about 30% of French origin; some 23% is of other European origin, principally Irish, German, Ukrainian, Scandinavian, Italian, Dutch, and Polish; 2% Indian and Eskimo; and less than 1% Asian; **Population Distribution:** 73.6% urban; **Density:** 5.6 inhabitants per sq. mi.

Largest Cities (M.A. = Metropolitan Area): (1967 estimates) Montreal 1,222,255 (M.A. 2,489,000); Toronto 664,584 (M.A. 2,233,000); Vancouver 410,375 (M.A. 923,000); Edmonton 376,925 (M.A. 412,000), Hamilton 298,121 (M.A. 463,000); Ottawa 290,741 (M.M.A. 508,000); Winnipeg 257,005 (M.A. 514,000); London 194,416 (M.A. 215,000); Windsor 192,544 (M.A. 217,000); Quebec 166,984 (M.A. 419,000).

Per Capita Income: $3,092 (1970); **Gross National Product (GNP):** $84.4 billion (1970); **Economic Statistics:** Manufacturing accounts for about 25% of GNP (chief industries: motor vehicles, pulp and paper, meat processing, petroleum refining, iron and steel mills, automotive parts, dairy factories, sawmills and planing mills, machinery and equipment, smelting and refining); about 18% is derived from services; 23% from trade and finance; 5% from agriculture (wheat, tobacco, barley, vegetables, fruits, potatoes), animal husbandry, forestry, fishing; and trapping; **Minerals and Mining:** ,Crude petroleum, nickel, copper, iron ore, zinc, natural gas, asbestos, and lead are exploited in large quantities; **Labor Force:** 8,374,000 (1970), with 22.7% employed in manufacturing, 25.7% in services, 7.7% in agriculture. The average factory worker earns $550-$650 a month. The average monthly wage for agricultural workers is $245 with board; **Foreign Trade:** Exports, chiefly vehicles and parts, newsprint paper, nickel, copper, and aluminum ores and alloys, woodpulp, wheat, lumber, and crude petroleum, totaled $16.8 billion in 1970. Imports, chiefly motor vehicles and parts, nonfarm machinery, steel, crude petroleum, aircraft and parts, communications, electrical, and scientific equipment, textiles, and chemicals, totaled $13.9 billion; **Principal Trade Partners:** United States, Britain, Japan, West Germany, Venezuela, The Netherlands, Australia, Italy, France.

Vital Statistics: Birthrate, 17.6 per 1,000 of pop.; death rate, 7.3; **Life Expectancy:** 72 years; **Health Statistics:** 105 inhabitants per hospital bed; 717 per physician; **Infant Mortality:** 19.3 per 1,000 births; **Illiteracy:** 0-3%; **Education Statistics:** 17,069 primary and secondary schools, with combined enrollment of 5,701,400; **Enrollment in Higher Education:** ,479,961; **GNP Expended on Education:** 8.6%.

Transportation: Surfaced roads total 396,098 mi.; **Motor Vehicles:** ,8,254,160 (1969); **Passenger Cars:** 6,433,283 (1969); **Railway Mileage:** ,59,115; **Ports:** Sept Iles, Vancouver, Montreal, Thunder Bay, Cartier, Hamilton, Halifax, Quebec, Toronto, Saint John; **Major Airlines:** Air Canada, the governmet line, and Canadian Pacific Airlines, a private carrier, operate domestic and international services; **Communications:** Both government and privately owned; **Radio Stations:** ,389; **Receivers:** About 10.5 million; **Television Stations:** 128; **Receivers:** 7.7 million; **Telephones:** 9,296,048; **Newspapers:** 120 dailies, about 214 copies per 1,000 inhabitants.

Weights and Measures: British standards are used; **Travel Requirements:** (1971) Proof of citizenship, onward ticket.

FRANCE

Area: 211,208 sq. mi.; Population: 50,890,000 (1970 est.).

Official Name: French Republic; Capital: Paris; Nationality: French; Languages: French is the official and predominant language. Other languages spoken include Breton (akin to Welsh) in
brittany; a German dialect in Alsace and Lorraine; Flemish in north-
eastern France; Spanish, Catalan, and Basque in the southwest, and
Italian in the southeast and on the island of Corsica; Religion: The
vast majority of the population is Roman Catholic; about 2% is
Protestant and 1% Jewish. Moslems, mostly immigrants from North
Africa, number about 500,000; Flag: A tricolor of blue, white, and
red vertical stripes; Anthem: La Marseillaise; Currency: Franc (5.51
per U.S. $1).

Location: Western Europe. France is bounded on the north by the
English Channel and the Strait of Dover; on the northeast of the
North Sea, Belgium and Luxembourg; on the east by Germany, Swit-
zerland, and Italy; on the southeast by the Mediterranean Sea; on the
south by Andorra and Spain; and on the west by the Atlantic Ocean;
Features: About two-thirds of the country consists of flat or gently
rolling terrain, and the remaining third is mountainous. A broad plain
covers most of northern and western France, from the Belgian border
in the northeast to Bayonne in the southwest. The lowland plains
area is bounded on the south by the Pyrenees; on the southeast by
the mountainous Massif Central; and on the east by the Alps, Spree
and Vosges mountains; Chief Rivers: Seine, Loire, Garonne, Paone,
Rhine.

Head of State and of Government: President Georges Pompidou,
born 1911, elected 1969. In addition to the president,the executive
branch of the government is composed of a council of ministers
headed by the premier, Jacques Chaban-Delmas, born 1915, appointed by the president 1969; Effective Date of Present Constitution: 1958; Legislative Body: Parliament (bicameral), consisting of
the National Assembly and the Senate. The National Assembly,
elected by direct universal suffrage for 5 years, is composed of 487
members. The Senate is composed of 283 members, elected indir-
ectly for 9 years by an electoral college made up of National
Assembly members, the General Departmental Councils, and the

delegates of the Municipal Councils. The National Assembly can be dissolved by the president with the advice of the premier; **Local Government**: Metropolitan France is divided into 95 departments, each headed by a prefect appointed by the central government and each under the authority of a popularly elected General Council. The departments are divided into cantons and communes, with each commune electing its own municipal council.

Ethnic Composition: The French are a mixture of the 3 basic European stocks: Nordic, Alpine, and Mediterranean. The largest foreign-born groups are North Africans, Italians, Spaniards, Czechoslovaks, Poles, and Yugoslavs; **Population Distribution**: 63% urban, 37% rural; **Density**: 248 inhabitants per sq. mi.

Largest Cities (M.A. = Metropolitan Area): (1968 estimates) Paris 2,590,771 (M.A. 8,196,746); Marseilles 889,029 (M.A. 964,412); Lyons 527,800 (M.A. 1,074,823); Toulouse 370,796 (M.A. 439,764); Nice 322,442 (M.A. 392,635); Bordeaux 266,662 (M.A. 555,152); Nantes 259,208 (M.A. 393,731); Strasbourg 249,396 (M.A. 334,668).

Per Capita Income: $2,783 (1969); **Gross National Product (GNP)**: $140 billion (1969); **Economic Statistics**: About 35% of GNP comes from industry (metalworking, machinery, chemicals, transport equipment, food and beverages, textiles, clothing); 14% from wholesale and retail services; 10% from construction; 8% from agriculture (wheat, barley, potatoes, beet sugar, apples, wine, beef cattle, and pigs); and the rest from other activities; **Minerals and Mining**: The country is an important producer of iron ore, potash, bauxite, coal, natural gas, sulphur, and building raw materials. It also has deposits of zinc, lead, pyrites, phosphates, and uranium; **Labor Force**: 20.6 million, with about 28% in manufacturing, 32% in trade and services, 16% in agriculture, fishing, and forestry, 12% in public services and administration, and 10% in building and public works. The average factory worker earns about $125 a month; **Foreign Trade**: Exports, chiefly machinery, chemicals, textiles, automobiles, steel, grain, and aircraft, totaled $15.1 billion in 1969. Imports, mainly machinery, foodstuffs, petroleum, chemicals, steel, nonferrous metals, and transportation equipment, totaled $17.4 billion; **Principal Trade Partners**: West Germany, Belgium, Luxembourg, Italy, United States, Switzerland, Britain, Netherlands, Algeria.

Vital Statistics: Birthrate, 16.7 per 1,000 of pop.; death rate, 11.3; Life Expectancy: 71 years; Health Statistics: 150 inhabitants per hospital bed, 770 per physician; Infant Mortality: 16.4 per 1,000 births; Illiteracy: 0-3%; Education Statistics: 89,953 primary and secondary schools, with combined enrollment of 7,851,000 pupils; Enrollment in Higher Education: 643,000; GNP Expended on Education: 4.6%.

Transportation: Surfaced roads total 485,000 mi.; Motor Vehicles: 14,650,800 (1969); Passenger Cars: 12 million (1969); Railway Mileage: 22,940; Ports: Marseilles, Le Havre, Dunkirk, Nantes, St. Nazaire, Rouen, Bordeaux; Major Airlines: Air France and UTA operate international flights; Air-Inter operates domestic flights; Communications: State controlled; Radio Stations: 14; Receivers: 15,796,000 (1969); Television Stations: 2; Receivers: 10,121,000 (1969); Telephones: 8,114,041 (1969); Newspapers: 109 dailies, 243 copies per 1,000 inhabitants.

Weights and Measures: Metric system; Travel Requirements: Passport, no visa for 3 months.

CONGO (BRAZZAVILLE)

Area: 132,046 sq. mi.; **Population:** 915,000 (1969 est.).

Official Name: People's Republic of the Congo; **Capital:** Brazzaville; **Nationality:** Congolese; **Languages:** French is the official language; Lingala and Kongo are the principal spoken languages; **Religion:** 50% animist, 49% Christian (mainly Roman Catholic), and 1% Moselm; **Flag:** A red field; in the upper left corner is a yellow 5-pointed star above crossed yellow hammer and hoe, surrounded by green palm branches; **Anthem:** The Internationale; **Currency:** Franc (277.7 per U.S. $1).

Location: West-central Africa. The People's Republic of the Congo is bordered on the north by Cameroon and the Central African Republic, on the east and south by the Democratic Republic of the Congo (Kinshasa), on the southwest by Cabinda, a portion of the Portuguese territory of Angola, and the Atlantic Ocean, and on the west by Gabon and Cameroon; **Features:** The country consists of a low-lying coastal zone, then alternating highlands and a plateau. Roughly half the land area is covered by dense equatorial forest, and a quarter of the country covered by marshes; **Chief Rivers:** Congo, Oubangui.

Head of State and of Government: President Marien Ngouabi, born 1937, seized power in an army-led coup in August 1968. As president of the Congolese Labor Party, established by the constitution of January 3, 1970, Ngouabi is automatically head of state; he also is president of the Council of State, the nation's ruling body; **Effective Date of Present Constitution:** January 3, 1970; **Legislative Body:** None. Legislation is the responsibility of the Political Bureau of the Congolese Labor Party; **Local Government:** Municipal, prefectural, and subprefectural councils.

Ethnic Composition: The population is predominantly Bantu; the principal groupings include the Bacongo, Bateke, M'Bochi, and Sangha. Pygmies number about 5,000; of some 12,000 Europeans most are French; **Population Distribution:** 39% urban; **Density:** 7 inhabitants per sq. mi.

Largest Cities: (1969 estimates). Brazzaville 150,000, Pointe-Noire 90,000.

Per Capita Income: $200 (1968 est.); Gross National Product (GNP): $174 million (1968 est.); Economic Statistics: About a third of production is from agriculture, forestry, and fishing; main cash and food crops are peanuts, palm kernels, coffee, cocoa, bananas, sugarcane, rice, corn, manioc, and sweet potatoes. Industry is concentrated in forest products and food processing (sugar refining, palm and peanut oil, brewing, flour milling). Mining, transportation, power, government and other services account for the rest of output; Minerals and Mining: large deposits of high-grade potash are expected to raise export proceeds well above that of decreasing crude petroleum production. There are high-grade iron-ore reserves; small amounts of gold and lead are mined; Labor Force: About 50% of the population is economically active, with about 60% of the labor force engaged in subsistence agriculture; Foreign Trade: Exports, chiefly wood and industrial diamonds, totaled $44 million in 1969. Imports, mainly machinery and electrical equipment, vehicles and parts, textiles and clothing, mineral products, and chemicals, totaled $83 million; Principal Trade Partners: France, West Germany, Netherlands, Britain, United States.

Vital Statistics: Estimated birthrate, 44.4 per 1,000 of pop.; estimated death rate, 22.8; Life Expectancy: 37 years; Health Statistics: 170 inhabitants per hospital bed; 8,350 per physician (1967); Infant Mortality: 180 per 1,000 births; Illiteracy: 80%; Education Statistics: 950 primary and secondary schools, with combined enrollment of 237,371 pupils (1968); Enrollment in Higher Education: 1,485 (1968); GNP Expended on Education: N.A.

Transportation: Surfaced roads total 985 mi.; Motor Vehicles: 9,000 (1969); Passenger Cars: N.A.; Railway Mileage: 500; Ports: Pointe-Noire is the main sea outlet; Brazzaville is the main river port; Major Airlines: Air Congo and Lina Congo operate internal services; Air Afrique, Aeroflot, Air France. KLM, Sabena, and UTA operate services to Brazzaville; Communications: State controlled; Radio Stations: 2; Receivers: 62,000 (1969); Television Stations: 1; Receivers: 500 (1969); Telephones: 9,812 (1969); Newspapers: 3 dailies, 1.3 copies per 1,000 inhabitants.

Weights and Meausres: Metric system; Travel Requirements: (1971) Passport, visa valid for 2 months, $5 fee, 2 pictures, financial guarantee, police certificate.

ECUADOR

Area: 109,483 sq. mi.; Population: 6,194,000 (1970 est.).

Official Name: Republic of Ecuador; Capital: Quito; National-ity: Ecuadorean; Languages: Spanish, the official language, is spoken by about 93% of the population, and Quechua by 7%; Reli-gion: Overwhelmingly Roman Catholic; Flag: Half the width of the flag is yellow and the remaining half consists of blue and red bands; in the center is the national coat of arms; Anthem: Hail, O Father-land; Currency: Sucre (25.25 per U.S. $1).

Location: South America. Crossed by the Equator, from which the country gets its name, Ecuador is bordered on the north by Colom-bia, on the east and south by Peru, and on the west by the Pacific Ocean. The Galapagos islands, some 600 miles west of the mainland, are part of the national territory; Features: About a fourth of the country consists of a coastal plain, and another fourth of the Sierra, or highlands, lying between two chains of the Andes Mountains. The Oriente, or eastern jungle, covers the remaining half of the country; Chief Rivers: Guayas, Esmeraldas.

Head of State and of Government: President Jose Maria Velasco Ibarra, born 1893, elected 1968; assumed dictatorial powers in 1970 for the remainder of his 4-year term expiring August 1972; Effective Date of Present Constitution: The 1967 constitution was voided by Velasco when he disbanded Congress in 1970. Proposed amendments to the 1946 constitution have been drawn up; Legislative Body: The National Congress (bicameral), consisting of a Senate and a Chamber of Deputies, was dissolved in 1970. A new Congress is scheduled for election concurrently with the President in June 1972; Local Govern-ment: 19 provinces, each headed by a governor appointed by the president.

Ethnic Composition: 40% Indian, 40% mestizo, 10% of European (chiefly Spanish) origin, 10% Negro; Population Distribution: 46% urban; Density: 56 inhabitants per sq. mi.

Largest Cities: (1967 estimates) Guayaquil 680,209, Quito 462,863.

Per Capita Income: $213 (1970); Gross National Product (GNP): $1.54 billion (1970); Economic Statistics: 31.2% of GNP is derived from agriculture (bananas, coffee, cocoa, rice, sugar, cotton, grains, fruits and vegetables), forestry, and fishing; 16.9% from manufacturing (textiles, food processing, petroleum refining, cement); 14.1% from trade and finance; 10.6% from services; **Minerals and Mining:** Petroleum is the primary mineral product. There are large deposits of calcium carbonate and copper; small quantities of gold are mined; **Labor Force:** 1,940,900 (1970), of which more than half is employed in agriculture, and 14% in manufacturing; **Foreign Trade:** Exports, chiefly bananas, coffee, and cocoa, totaled $201.4 million in 1970. Imports, mainly machinery, transportation equipment, chemicals, and paper products, totaled $242.9 million; **Principal Trade Partners:** United States, West Germany, Japan, Britain, Italy, Colombia, Canada.

Vital Statistics: Estimated birthrate, 44.9 per 1,000 of pop.; estimated death rate, 11.4; **Life Expectancy:** 52 years; **Health Statistics:** 260 inhabitants per hospital bed; 1,580 per physician; **Infant Mortality:** 86.1 per 1,000 births; **Illiteracy:** 32%; **Education Statistics:** 8,192 primary and secondary schools, with combined enrollment of 1,170,162 pupils; **Enrollment in Higher Education:** 33,562; **GNP Expended on Education:** 4% (1968).

Transportation: Surfaced roads total 1,174 mi.; **Motor Vehicles:** 59,500 (1969); **Passenger Cars:** 25,500 (1969); **Railway Mileage:** 727; **Ports:** Guayaquil, Puerta Bolivan, Manta, Bahia de Caraquez, La Libertad, Esmeraldas; **Major Airlines:** AREA and Ecuatoriana de Aviacion operate internal and international flights; **Communications:** Both government and privately owned; **Radio Stations:** 247; **Receivers:** 1,200,000 (1969); **Television Stations:** 14; **Receivers:** 71,000 (1968); **Telephones:** 94,658 (1970); **Newspapers:** 25 dailies, 42 copies per 1,000 inhabitants (1969).

Weights and Measures: Metric system is official but Spanish measures are generally used; **Travel Requirements:** Proof of citizenship, tourist card, $2 fee, 2 pictures, onward ticket.

ISBN 0—8403—0783—